First I win a contest that
makes me a TV star.
Then I get to do some of
the most awesome extreme
sports in the world. And my
two best friends get
to come along for the ride.
How lucky am I?

First published in Great Britain in 2005 by
RISING STARS UK LTD.
76 Farnaby Road, Bromley, BR1 4BH

First published in Australia by Scholastic Australia in 2004.
Text copyright © Philip Kettle, 2004.

A Black Hills book, produced by black dog books

Designed by Blue Boat Design
Cover photo: Blue Boat Design

For more information visit our website at:
www.risingstars-uk.com

British Library Cataloguing in Publication Data

A CIP record for this book is available from the British Library

ISBN 1 905056 42 7

Printed by Bookmarque Ltd, Croydon, Surrey

# THE XTREME WORLD OF BILLY KOOL

by Phil Kettle

## book:03
## bungy jumping

## RISING ★ STARS

# CONTENTS

Something To
Look Forward To      1.

The Dream      4.

The Dance      9.

Cast and Crew Meeting      16.

The Jump      19.

Lights, Camera, Action      26.

The Wrap Up      45.

Extreme Information      48.

# BUNGY JUMPING EQUIPMENT

### Ankle Harness

The ankle harness straps around your ankles. It is then connected to the bungy cord.

### Chest and Waist Harness

The chest and waist harness is a full body harness that supports the body more than the ankle harness. This harness is great for people with knee or ankle injuries, or for older people.

### Bungy Cord

The bungy cord is
an elastic rope that
connects you to the
platform that you jump
from, via your harness.

### Bungy Helmet

A helmet is used
as a safety measure
in case an accident
occurs.

## SOMETHING TO LOOK FORWARD TO

The biggest disappointment about weekends is that they come to an end. It would be much better if we went to school on the weekend and had the rest of the week off. At the moment the only good thing about Mondays is that I am one day closer to another extreme sport.

Whitewater rafting was awesome. I was really looking forward to going bungy jumping on the weekend too. At least, I was until

I started imagining what it would be like to jump off a bridge.

Nathan thinks about school in a similar way to me. He says schooldays are something that keep the weekends separated!

Sally is different to us. Sally says that school is an extreme brain adventure. I think of it more as a brain strain. I suppose that's why Sally's marks are always a lot better than Nathan's and mine.

On Monday nights, I try to get most of my schoolwork done. That means that for the rest of the week the workload isn't as bad.

But no matter how hard I try, I still like the things I do away from

school a lot more than the things
I do at school. Let's face it—who
would rather be at school if they had
their own TV show?

THE DREAM

This week, school was going to be
a little bit different. Our school had
a disco once a term and it was this
Thursday night.

At the other discos we'd been to,
Nathan and I sat in the corner of the
hall. Neither of us was game enough
to get up and dance. Instead we told
each other that only nerds dance.
Sally always danced with other girls.
That is such a girl thing to do.

This disco was going to be

different. We were popular now.
Nathan and I weren't called little
nerds anymore by the older kids.
They now called us those lucky little
nerds who have their own television
show.

One of the girls in my class had
even asked me for my autograph.
At first I wasn't sure whether she
was making fun of me or whether
she was serious. I signed her school
diary anyway.

There is a new girl in our class.
Her name is Roz. She's the hottest
girl that I've ever seen, except
for Crystal, Nathan's older sister.
Crystal had only spoken to me twice
in the last twelve months so I figured

that there wasn't much chance that she would dance with me.

But Roz had only moved to our school one month ago and she had already spoken to me. 'You're on that television show — *The Xtreme World of Billy Kool*,' she said. 'That's a funny name, Billy Kool.'

I didn't know what to say, but it didn't matter because she kept talking.

'What sport are you doing next?' she asked.

'Bungy jumping, this weekend,' I said.

'I went bungy jumping in New Zealand,' she said. 'It was awesome. Are you scared?'

'No way,' I lied. 'I can't wait.'

'I've got to go,' she said. 'I might see you at the disco.'

On the way home I told Nathan about talking with Roz. 'I'm going to ask her to dance,' I said. 'When she smiles it's like the whole room lights up.'

'That must be the light reflecting off her braces,' Nathan said.

Sally caught up with us. 'What are you talking about?' she asked.

'Bungy jumping,' I said straight away.

'It's going to be unreal,' said Sally.

'Yeah, we'll feel what it's like to be a bird,' said Nathan.

'Yeah, a bird whose wings have fallen off,' I said.

I went to sleep on Monday night dreaming about jumping from a bridge with a huge rubber band wrapped around my ankles. Before I woke up I dreamed that I was at the dance wearing swimming trunks, my face covered in zinc cream and water dripping from me.

Both dreams seemed more like nightmares to me. I dreamed them again on Tuesday night and Wednesday night.

# THE DANCE

I didn't think there could be
anything worse than being woken
up by your mum telling you that
you're going to be late for school.
But there is something worse.
What's worse is when you go into
the bathroom, have a shower, then
stand in front of the bathroom
mirror and wipe the steam away.
The mirror clears and your brain
seems to wake at the same time.

Could this be true? I wiped

the mirror again. How could this happen to me? My heart started to pound harder and faster than I imagined it would when we were standing at the top of the bridge, about to bungy jump.

On the end of my nose was the biggest and reddest spot I had ever seen. It was like a volcano ready to explode. It was as big as the rest of my nose. Of all the days to have a volcano poke its ugly head out of my face. I pushed my face a little closer to the mirror. The volcano needed just a little help to erupt. I put my forefinger and thumb either side of the volcano, shut my eyes and squeezed.

Lava, steam, ash exploded—
nobody would be safe. I was sure
that I could hear people yelling,
'Run for your lives or you'll be
drowned in lava.' I opened my
eyes. Tears were running down my
cheeks—tears of pain.

The mirror was covered in ash and
lava. It would be a big job to clean
it. I was pleased that I had to go to
school.

When I went to the kitchen for
breakfast, Mum said, 'Having
spots is part of growing up. It's just
something that you just have to put
up with.'

That didn't make me feel much
better. How could I go to the dance

looking like I was wearing a clown's nose? What if the spot just kept building up and erupted again in the middle of the dance? If that happened, I might drown everybody in spot lava and there couldn't be a worse way of dying than that!

That evening, Mum managed to cover the volcano with some make-up. Sally's mum arrived at my place just after six o'clock. She was the designated driver. Nathan, Sally and I sat in the back seat on the way to the disco. We never said much—it wasn't that cool to talk about things that we did in front of our parents.

Sally looked really grown up.

She'd changed a lot in the last few months. I wasn't too sure what it was, but she looked different.

We walked into the hall. Lights were flashing and music was pumping. The hall was already crowded. Sally walked straight onto the dance floor and started to dance with her girlfriends.

Nathan and I walked to the corner of the hall and sat on the same seats that we always did. It was hard to see in the lights. But there she was, like a lighthouse on a dark and stormy night, in the middle of the floor dancing away.

'There's Roz,' Nathan said. 'Her teeth are really gleaming. They could have used her mouth instead of a mirror ball.'

I decided to ask her to dance. At least my face would be so red she wouldn't be able to see the volcano on my nose. Just when I had built up the courage to walk over to her, Nathan nudged me in the ribs.

'Hey, who's she dancing with?'

I wasn't sure whether I was disappointed or relieved. Roz was dancing with one of the older kids. Their heads were bent close together. I wondered if they were whispering to each other. There was no way I could ever be that close to her without bumping into her.

Maybe it was better that I just

kept pretending about Crystal.

'Hey, you two, what are doing sitting there? Come and dance, Billy.'

It was Crystal.

I danced with her twice! The only words that I managed to say were, 'Thanks very much.' Then Crystal said that she had to go and meet her friends.

When I got back to Nathan, he said, 'Glad it was you that had to dance with her. She's so embarrassing.'

It was the best disco that I have ever been to.

CAST AND
CREW MEETING

When Friday came, butterflies flew
into my stomach. I tried to ignore
them when we sat in the cast and
crew meeting. There was a map of
the bungy location on the wall.
The first assistant director told us
we were jumping from a bridge.
There was a 45-metre drop to
the water below. We'd be pulled
down into a boat when we stopped
bouncing in the air. The butterflies
started fluttering like crazy.

'My mother asked me whether she should put some glue in my cereal to help keep it down,' Nathan whispered.

'Yeah, well my dad wanted to know whether I had any plastic underpants,' I whispered.

'You're both worried about nothing. I can't wait to jump,' said Sally.

'The limo will pick you up at 8 a.m.,' the director said. 'We'll run through safety checks with Shey. While we're doing that, the camera crew are going to set up, and you'll be wired for sound. There will be two cameras positioned on the bridge. One on the boat, and we're going to attach a camera to your clothes, so we can get some extreme close-ups of your expressions and the jump. No one's scared of heights, are they?' The director laughed.

I didn't think much of his sense of humour.

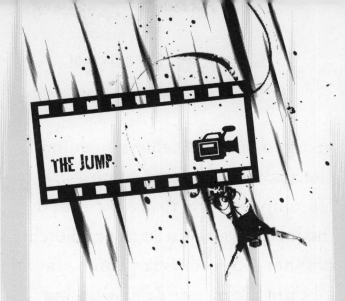

THE JUMP

'Here we go,' said Sally as the limo pulled up at the bungy jumping site the next morning.

'Yep, this is where we get to find out what a bird feels like when it's flying along and its wings stop working,' said Nathan.

'At least we've got a rope tied to our legs,' I said.

I tried to distract myself by thinking about what I had to say when the cameras started to roll.

We'd been in the television studio every afternoon after school, learning and practising our lines.

When we got out of the car, the director was ordering people around all over the place. He saw us and said, 'Come on, guys, the light is just right. Go to the caravan, we've got clothes we want you to wear.'

We put on T-shirts that said *The Xtreme World of Billy Kool*. Shey and the instructors ran through all the safety checks with us, while the camera crew set up. Then the sound crew attached microphones to our T-shirts and gave us earplug receivers to put in.

'Can you hear me? Testing.'

The voice of the director came
through the earpiece.

'I can hear you,' I said.

'I want you to listen very carefully
to what I have to say,' the director
said. 'This might seem like a lot of
fun to the three of you, but I can
tell you this is not called extreme
for nothing. You have to listen
to everything that is said to you!
Bungy jumping can be really
dangerous. Do I make myself clear?'

'Yes, sir,' the three of us said at the
same time.

'When I say so, the three of
you will walk to the middle of the
bridge. I want you to forget that the
cameras are on you. When you get

to the instructors, do exactly what they tell you. Billy, when you reach the instructors, turn toward me and announce the show. Just the same way that we practised in the studios. Are you ready? One, two, three, action!

We walked toward the centre of the bridge. The words 'one, two, three … normal conversation' came through the earpiece and at the same time I heard butterflies stampeding in my stomach which, I'm sure, everyone could hear. I just hoped they stayed in my stomach.

The voice of the producer came through my earpiece again.

'You're nearly at the centre of the

bridge. As soon as you get there, turn and face me and start the introduction. Remember, we want to get this right the first time. Good luck!'

# Location Map

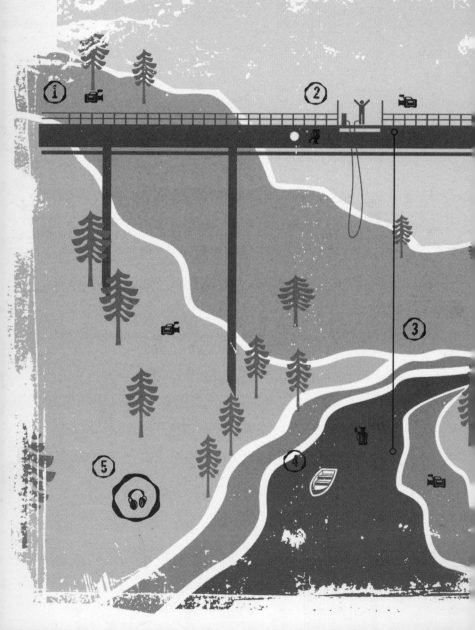

# Our Equipment

**Ankle Harness**

**Chest and Waist Harness**

**Bungy Cord**

**Bungy Helmet**

1. Director's position

2. Safety checkpoint and jumping platform

3. 45-metre jump

4. Boat with pole to pull you aboard

5. Sound crew based for monitoring

LIGHT'S, CAMERA, ACTION

## Billy

Hi. My name is Billy Kool. These are my friends, Sally and Nathan. We would like to welcome you to *The Xtreme World of Billy Kool*. Today's show is the third in this current series about extreme sports. Extreme sports mean taking your body and mind to their limits and doing things in sport that you would not normally do!

The first thing you should remember is that extreme sports should only ever be tried when expert supervision is available. Today we are up for a bungy jumping adrenaline rush. Here is our safety co-ordinator and the person in charge of the bungy jump, Shey.

**SHEY**
Well, hello to you, Billy Kool, Sally and Nathan. It's great to be part of your extreme world again. Today we're going to bungy jump. From the middle of the bridge to the water below is a 45-metre jump.

*BILLY, SALLY and NATHAN stand well back from the edge of the bridge. Sally keeps glancing over to the jumping platform, where the bungy operators are checking the equipment that will be used.*

**BILLY**
Should we look at the
water below?

**SHEY**
No! If you look below, it
might make you feel a bit
queasy and make it hard
for you to jump!

**NATHAN**
I feel as if I have a
million butterflies in my
stomach!

**SALLY**
As long as you keep them
in your stomach and don't
spit them out over me!

**SHEY**
Well, it's time for us
to get ready for the
first jump. We've already

weighed Billy, Nathan and
Sally.

**BILLY**
Yeah! We all weigh more
than forty-five kilograms,
which is the requirement
before you are allowed to
jump!

**SHEY**
That's right. When we know
what your exact weight
is, we adjust the length
of the rope to suit the
jumper. We've already got
the rope ready for the
first jumper. The boys
have said that Sally wants
to jump first.

**SALLY**
That's the first I've

heard of it. It sure shows how brave the boys are!

**NATHAN**
We were just being polite-girls first.

**SALLY**
Well, I've never heard you say that before!

**SHEY**
Sally, if you want to show the boys that girls really rule when it comes to extreme sports, come here and we'll put the attachments on and do a safety check.

*SHEY and the bungy operators check Sally's equipment. Sally looks a bit pale.*

**SHEY**
Calibration set.
Karabiner locked on.
Top system check.
Rigging check.
Jump systems are secure.
Are you ready, Sally?

**SALLY**
As ready as I ever will
be!

**SHEY**
Good. Take small steps
to the edge, keeping
your eyes on the horizon.
There's a boat waiting
for you at the end of your
jump. When I say, 'three,
two, one, bungy' just let
yourself fall into a dive.

**SALLY**
Okay.

**SHEY**
Three, two, one, bungy!

*Sally hesitates for a few seconds, then falls from the bridge.*

**SALLY**
Aaaaaaaahhhhh!

*Sally reaches the lowest point of the jump and is flung back up in the air.*

**SALLY**
Wow, that was awesome. I feel like a yoyo! This is the most amazing feeling ever!

*Sally speaks into her microphone, but her voice is distorted by the wind. Billy and Nathan find it hard to hear her.*

**NATHAN**
Billy and I would love
to see how Sally's doing,
but we really don't want
to look over the edge.
Billy's scared of heights.

**BILLY**
I'll be right behind you,
Nathan, if you want to go
and look.

**NATHAN**
Even if we didn't see Sally
jump, we really heard her.
We didn't need any sound
equipment for that!

**BILLY**
What were you thinking
when you jumped, Sally?

**SALLY**
At first I was thinking

that I really, really
hoped the bungy cord was
the right length. Then
when I bounced up, it felt
like I was flying.

**BILLY**
Cool!

**NATHAN**
Wait until we go
skydiving!

**SHEY**
When you stop moving,
Sally, the crew in the
boat will pass a pole to
you. Grab it and they will
pull you into the boat.
Ignore the boys, Sally.
That was a fantastic jump.

**BILLY**
Well, I guess it's our

turn. How are you feeling, Nathan?

**NATHAN**
If I said I was anything else but scared I'd be lying!

**SHEY**
Because you boys aren't as brave as Sally, you're going to jump together. While Billy and Nathan are having harnesses put on, I would like to explain that you can jump as a pair. Billy and Nathan's harnesses will be linked together.

**NATHAN**
Hope those butterflies stay where they are!

**BILLY**
So do I! I'm right beside
you and I don't want to
get covered in them!

**SHEY**
Right. Small steps to
the edge. Are you ready?
Three, two, one, bungy!

*Billy and Nathan tiptoe to
the edge of the platform,
arguing about which of
them will push off from
the platform.*

**BILLY**
I'll push us.

**NATHAN**
No way. I will.

**BILLY**
What about if we pushed
off at the same time?

**SHEY**
Stop arguing, you two.
I'll say it again. Three,
two, one...

**BILLY**
Are you ready?

**NATHAN**
Ready as I'll ever be.

*The boys push off from the
platform.*

**BILLY AND NATHAN**
Aaaaaaaahhhhhhhhhhh!

*The helmet cams that
they're wearing show the
surrounding landscape
from all different angles.
After a while, Billy's
helmet cam fixes on
Nathan's face.*

**BILLY**
This is unreal.

**NATHAN**
I don't know what I was
expecting it to be like,
but it wasn't this.

**SALLY**
What were you guys
thinking when you jumped?

**NATHAN**
I was hoping that no
butterflies popped out of
Billy's stomach.

**BILLY**
Same!

**SALLY**
I'm in the boat, but my
legs are still shaking.
That was crazy.

**SHEY**
The boys will be in the boat in a few moments, when they've stopped moving around. Well viewers, this is what bungy jumping is all about!

*Billy and Nathan stop bouncing around and are helped into the boat. Nathan's legs are shaking.*

**BILLY**
That was so cool. Standing here in the boat looking up at the bridge, it's hard to believe that we've just jumped from it! It's so high.

**NATHAN**
My butterflies are still all locked up.

**BILLY**
I'm really pleased about that! On behalf of Sally, Nathan and myself, Billy Kool, I hope that you have enjoyed our second extreme sport. See you next episode when we're snowboarding. Remember the best highs in life come from living to the extreme. Until our next show, I'm Billy Kool and you're not!

**DIRECTOR**
Cut!

*The camera crew stop shooting Billy, Nathan and Sally and start setting up to shoot footage of the platform and boat. They will stay at the location for another two days to get the shots they need.*

**DIRECTOR**
Good work, people.
I never thought you'd make it over the edge, Billy and Nathan. It'll make great TV, especially the bit where you argued.

**BILLY**
That's why we had the fight, of course.

**DIRECTOR**
Oh, of course.

**BILLY**
I think that I'm going to
do that again. And this
time on my own!

**NATHAN**
That's one of your better
ideas.

**BILLY**
I thought so.

**SALLY**
That was the best
adrenaline rush ever. Can
we go again?

**DIRECTOR**
Not until I have a go.

**SHEY**
And me too.

**NATHAN**
We're so lucky we won

pretty painful. With bungy jumping at least you know that you have a huge rubber band attached to your ankles. Maybe next time I go bungy jumping I'll keep my eyes open!

## Dear Billy

Could you please write to me and tell me how I can write to Sally? I think that Sally is really cute. I think that you are good too and so is Nathan.

## Miles, a fan of yours

PS Could you tell Sally that I have her picture on my wall. I'm sorry that I cut you and Nathan out of the picture, but Sally is definitely the best.

# Extreme Information

## History

Bungy jumping is believed to have begun on Pentecost Island, a small island in the South Pacific. Legend has it that there was a woman who was trying to escape her husband. She climbed a very tall tree, attempting to hide. When her husband discovered her hiding spot he climbed the tree after her. The woman escaped him by jumping out of the tree as he grabbed for her. He fell to his death but she had tied a springy vine to her ankles which stopped her from hitting the ground.

A ritual developed out of this legend. Originally only the women of the villages were involved, but eventually the men took over and the jumps became an offering to the gods for a good harvest.

Each year the men would build tall wooden jumping towers against the side of a hill. Some of these were up to twenty-seven metres high. The men would then clear all the rocks and debris away from the base of the towers and stir up the dirt so that if they hit the ground, the impact would be a little softer.

The men would tie carefully measured vines to their ankles and leap off the platforms. Their measurements were so precise that the vines would stop their fall just centimetres from the ground.

The first modern bungy jump took place in Oxford, England. On April

Fool's day, 1979, a group of university students who were members of the Oxford Dangerous Sports Club jumped off a suspension bridge eighty metres high. The ropes they used to tie themselves to the bridge were actually cords designed to halt jets landing on aircraft carriers. The students were immediately arrested, but the idea caught on. Bungy jumps even took place off the Golden Gate Bridge in San Francisco, and the world's highest suspension bridge over Royal Gorge in Colorado.

In 1987, a New Zealand man named A. J. Hackett bungy jumped off the Eiffel Tower. The following year he returned to New Zealand to open the world's first commercial bungy jumping operation.

# Glossary

**Bungy**

The word bungy is New Zealand slang for 'elastic strap'.

**Butterflies**

When your stomach begins to churn.

**Harness**

Connects the bungy rope to the jumper's body.

**Jumper**

The person who is making the jump.

**Platform**

A solid, flat surface which sticks out over the edge of the bridge or structure that the jumper is leaping from. The jump takes place from the platform.

## Sandbagging

Jumpers hold extra weight as they fall, then release it just as they reach the bottom-most point of the jump. This means that they will spring back upwards much further than they would have with just their own body-weight. Sometimes, jumpers will actually use another person to provide the extra weight. This can be very dangerous because if the person doesn't let go at the precise moment, they will be flung into the air with the jumper.

## Wet head

When the jumper's head touches the water at the end of the jump.

# Equipment

### Bungy Cords

There are two main types of bungy cords—sheathed cords and all-rubber cords.

Sheathed cords were the first cords used in bungy jumping. They have a rubber core encased in a cotton or nylon sheath. They were originally designed to connect parachutes with heavy equipment being dropped from planes.

All-rubber cords are comprised of over 1000 individual strands of rubber tied together into one solid cord. All-rubber cords can stretch to four times their resting length during a jump. They were developed in New Zealand.

### Ankle Harness

An ankle harness is used by beginner jumpers. It is the most common harness system used in bungy jumping.

### Chest and Waist Harness

A chest and waist harness produces the least amount of stress on your body. With these harnesses, the cord is connected to your body very close to your centre of gravity/rotation.

### Bungy Knot

A bungy knot is another type of harness. A towel is wrapped around the jumper's legs for padding, then a loop of webbing is tied around the ankles.

# PHIL KETTLE

Phil Kettle lives in inner-city Melbourne, Australia. He has three children, Joel, Ryan and Shey. Originally from northern Victoria, Phil grew up on a vineyard. He played football and cricket and loved any sport where he could kick, hit or throw something.

These days, Phil likes to go to the Melbourne Cricket Ground on a winter afternoon and cheer on his favourite Australian Rules team, the Richmond Tigers. Phil hopes that one day he will be able to watch the Tigers win a grand final—'Even if that means I have to live till I'm 100.'

# THE XTREME WORLD OF BILLY KOOL

by Phil Kettle

01 All or Nothing
02 Whitewater Rafting
03 Bungy Jumping
04 Snowboarding
05 Skydiving
06 Mountain Biking
07 Kart Racing
08 Rock Climbing

Billy Kool books are available
from most booksellers.
For mail order information
please call Rising Stars on
01933 443862 or visit
www.risingstars-uk.com